I0844968

The
Ins-and-Outs
of
Over-and-Under
in
Adobe
Illustrator

How to Interlace Objects

Victor Langer

Copyright © 2021 Victor Langer
All rights reserved.
Excerpts in articles or reviews
are allowed.
ISBN 9798594966871

Victor Langer is a
graphic designosaur
specializing in logo design.
He has been in graphic design
for 50 years
and has been an
Adobe Illustrator fanatic
for 22 years.

Contents

Introduction

With detailed step-by-step exercises this book shows you how to create the over-and-under effect in Adobe Illustrator. That means how to make intersecting objects or parts of objects look like they are going over or under each other. This is especially useful in logo design, but can be used for any simple illustrations for any purpose. This is an intermediate level book and is not for beginners. It assumes that you know the basic moves in Illustrator.

Good Working Practices

- **Color:** Work in a light gray. Don't work in black or a dark color because it's hard to see your anchor points and Smart Guides indicators. Add color after the design is done.

- **Zoom Level:** Work at 100% zoom except to zoom in temporarily to edit fine details. If you work at other zoom levels the tools are hard to control.

- **Save Intermediates:** Before you make any significant changes to a design, move a copy down and work on the copy thus preserving intermediate designs, which you may need later if things don't work out and you have to start again from an earlier point. Work in a column, with earlier work at the top and later work at the bottom. Always do this before Outlining Strokes or doing Pathfinder > Unite.

- **Etc:** Do the exercises in the order given. They go from easy to hard. "Select" means use the Selection Tool, unless I specify a different selection tool. For the two modifier keys that differ on Mac and Windows, I give the Mac version first: Option/Alt and Command/Control.

The Basic Principle
Two Letters S

1. Make an S like so with two half circles and lines that are joined. The size of the image should be about 3-1/2" wide at 100% zoom. Use a stroke width of 20 points.

2. Rotate a copy 90°. Use the Rotate Tool. (The Bounding Box can't rotate *copies*.)

Outline Strokes (Object > Path > Outline Stroke). Remember to always move a copy down before you Outline Strokes, to preserve your intermediate images, which you may need to go back to later.

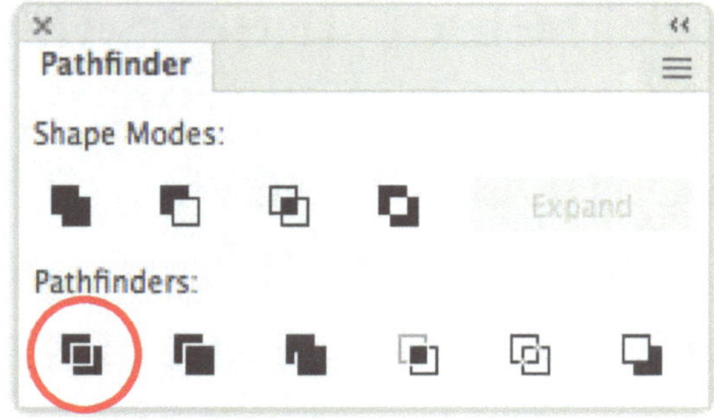

3. Select both objects. Show the Pathfinder Panel (Window > Pathfinder). In the Pathfinders section choose Divide. All intersecting areas are now separate objects, and are grouped.

4. Add a white stroke of 2 points so you can see where the divisions are. See what has happened? — The unpainted areas that were enclosed (islands) have also become objects. Here's how to prevent this:

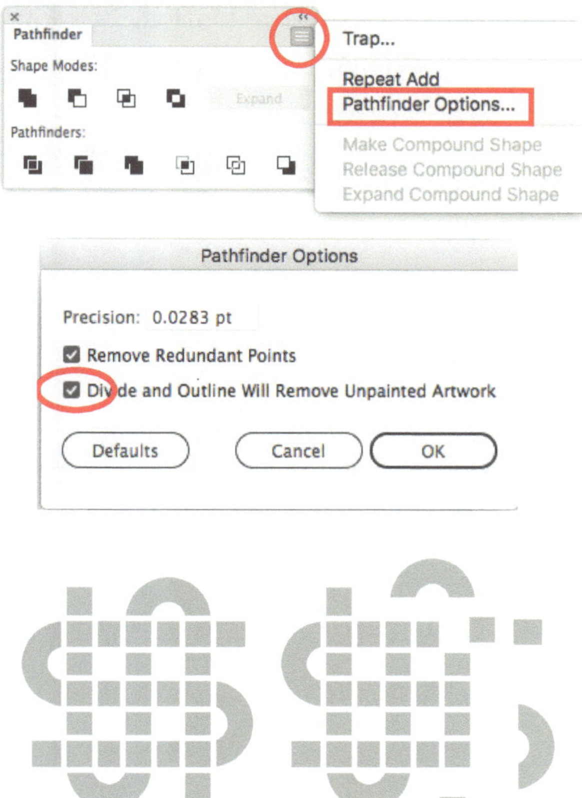

5. Start again with the object from step 2. This time, before Dividing, do this: In the Pathfinder Panel, in the flyout menu, choose Pathfinder Options, then check *Divide and Outline Will Remove Unpainted Artwork*. This prevents the enclosed areas from becoming objects. Now Divide again and add a 2 point white stroke so you can see the divisions. (Notice that you can pull the separate pieces apart with the Group Selection Tool.)

6. Now we can selectively reunite the pieces to give the illusion of over-and-under interlacing. Wherever you want one object to go **over** the other one you have to unite it with its two adjacent pieces. For example, working with the horizontal S, the pieces that are colored blue here would have to be united.

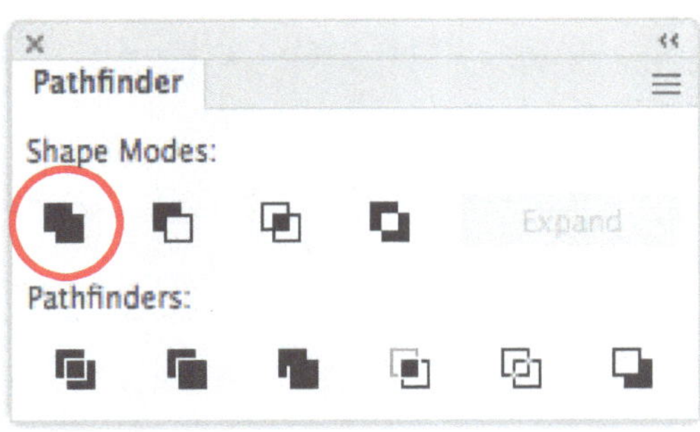

7. First, Ungroup the object, since it's automatically Grouped after Divide. Shift-select the objects shown in blue and then do Unite from the Pathfinder Panel, Shape Modes section. Disregard the long tool tip about using the Option/Alt key. We'll get to that later.

8. Repeat the process for the other S.

9. Rotate the design 45°. You can leave the white stroke, or use a different color stroke, or have no stroke and color the two Ss differently, or have a stroke and no fill. Done.

A Hanger Tangle

1. Draw this hanger. Use a 26 point stroke weight. Make it about 4″ wide at 100% zoom.

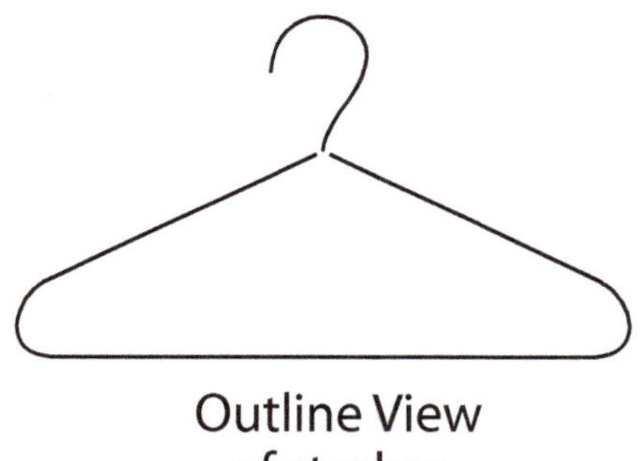

Outline View
of strokes

2. Move a copy down. Outline Strokes. Go to Outline View (View > Outline) to see the difference. Outline View always shows you the actual path. Always check it if you're not sure what you have.

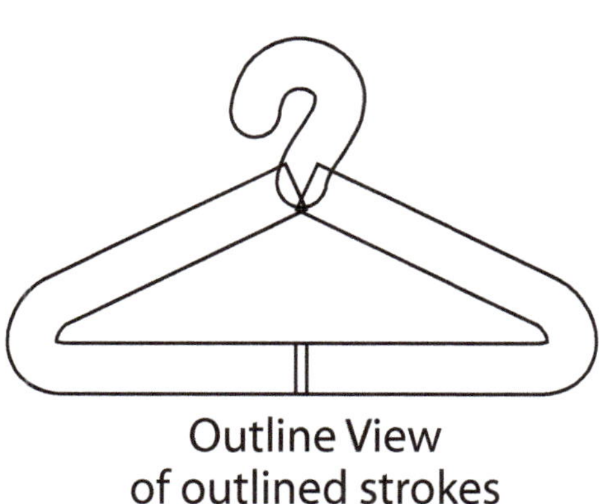

Outline View
of outlined strokes

Outline View
of united outlined strokes

3. Select the object, then do Pathfinder > Unite. Disregard the long tool tip for now. Check again in Outline View. You now have one unified object.

4. Rotate the object 45° clockwise. We want to rotate 4 more copies around in a ring, for a total of 5. This is a trial-and-error process. Draw a small circle of very light gray and place it where you think the center of the rotation might be.

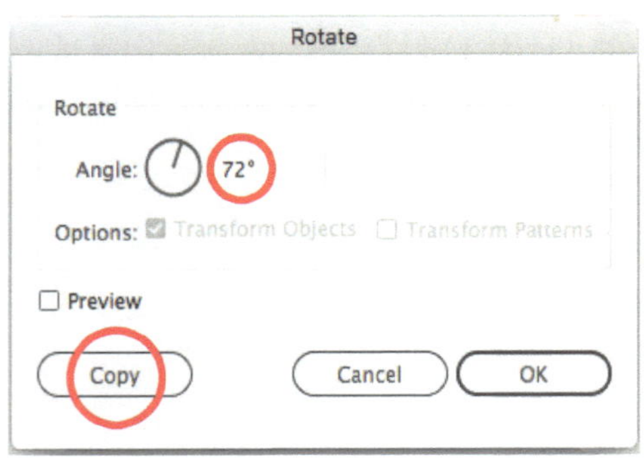

5. Select the object. Choose the Rotate tool. Position the Rotate tool cross hairs over the center of the circle. (This will be the center of rotation to try.) Option/Alt click. The Rotate Tool dialog will open. Put in the Angle of rotation. Since we want 5 designs total this will be 360 divided by 5 or 72°. Illustrator will do the math if you want. Put 360/5 in the Angle field. Then hit Copy. This is not a good intersection. Let's try moving the center point down and to the right.

6. That's close. Down a bit more.

7. That's good. Now hit Command/Control-D three times to get three more copies.

8. Delete the center point. Do Pathfinder > Divide as in Step 5 of the previous Exercise. Remember, before Dividing always see that the Option for *Divide and Outline Will Remove Unpainted Artwork* is checked.)

9. Then selectively Unite as in Steps 6 and 7 of the previous exercise.

10. Add final color.

You can leave the white stroke.

Or use a different color stroke.

Or have no stroke.

Or have a stroke with no fill.

Exercise 3
Finding the Center:
A Rotation Trick
A Ring of Stars

1. Draw a star like this. Use a 27 point stroke and make it about 3" wide at 100% zoom. Use Shift with the Star Tool to keep one point up. Dragging the Star Tool with Command/Control varies the pointyness. Then rotate it 180º. This will be the top star in the design.

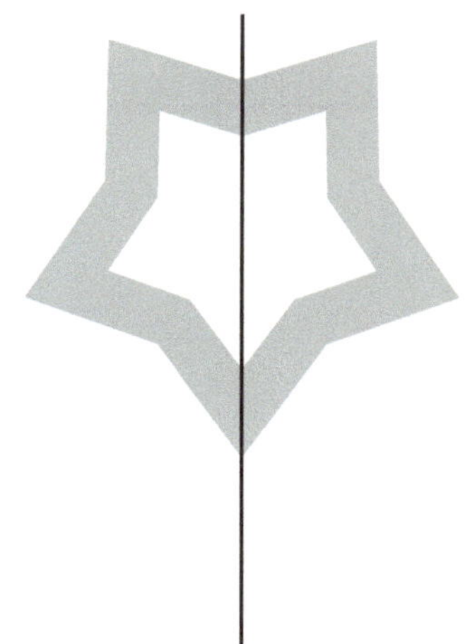

2. Instead of doing trial-and-error to find the best center point of the rotation, as in the previous Exercise, this is a better way. But it only works if a design is symmetrical and centered (left-to-right) with the center of rotation.

Draw a one point black stroke and center it on the star like so. Group them.

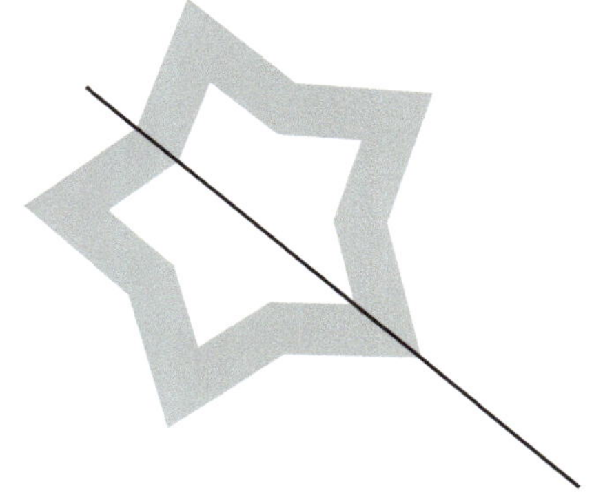

3. There are seven stars, so the angle of rotation will be 360/7º. Rotate a copy by this amount.

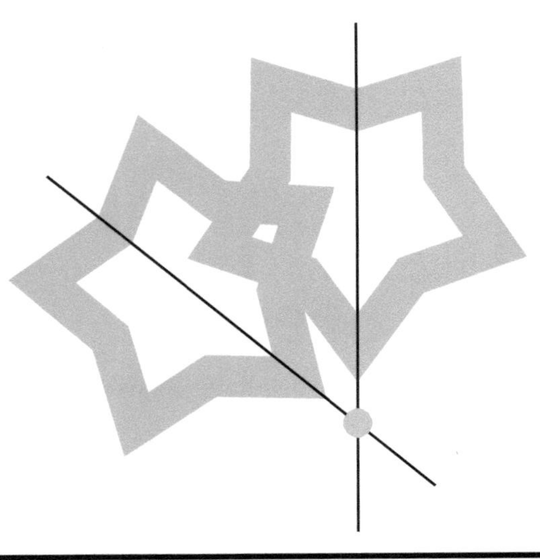

4. Overlap the two stars exactly the way you want them to intersect . With Smart Guides on, draw a small light gray circle exactly where the lines intersect.

5. Delete the lines. Outline Strokes on the stars.

6. With Smart Guides still on, select the star on the left, choose the Rotate tool, then roll over the circle until Smart Guides tells you you're on the center. Then Option/Alt click. This brings up the Rotate dialog. Put 360/7 in the Angle field. Click Copy. Then hit Command/Control-D five times to duplicate the move and get five more stars for a total of seven.

7. Delete the center point. Select all stars. Open the Pathfinder Panel. Make sure the Option for *Divide and Outline Will Remove Unpainted Artwork* is checked. Then Divide, and add a 2 point white stroke so you can see where the divisions are.

8. The object is grouped by default after Divide. Ungroup it. Start with the top star. As before, Shift-Select the piece that will go **over** along with its two neighbors. Color it to help you see it. (Shown in yellow here.) Then do Pathfinder > Unite as before.

9. Now do the same with the next star, going clockwise around the ring. Shown in green here. And so on, all the way around.

10. Add final color.

You can leave the white stroke.

Or use a different color stroke.

Or have no stroke.

Or have a stroke with no fill.

Five Square Interlace

Original object

Effect applied

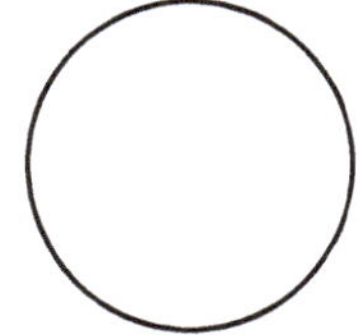

Outline View
of effect

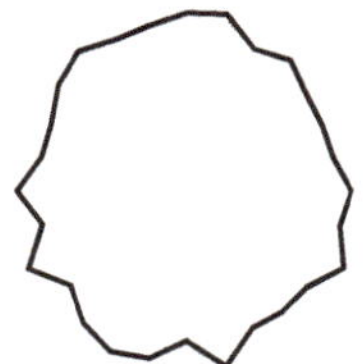

Outline View
of effect
after expanded

Before we do this exercise we have to talk about the difference between **paths**, **effects**, and **shapes**. A path is the basic drawn object. An effect is a visual appearance applied the object and is editable and reversible. It doesn't become part of the actual path of the object until you **expand** it (Object > Expand or Object > Expand Appearance).

Here's an example: Draw a circle with a color fill. Move a copy down. Apply a Roughen effect (Effect > Distort & Transform > Roughen). Then go to Outline View, which shows you the actual path. You see that the path is unchanged. Now move a copy down and expand it and see how it looks in Outline View.

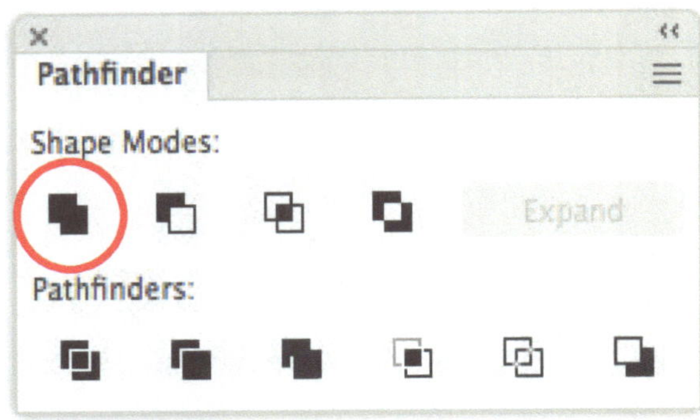

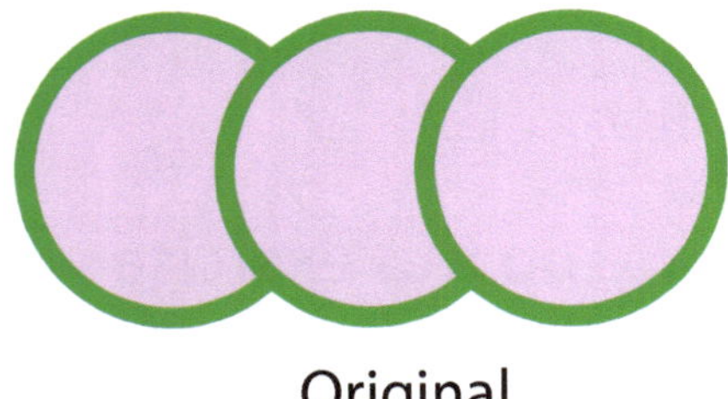

Original

Unite **without** Option/Alt
in Outline View
(= path)

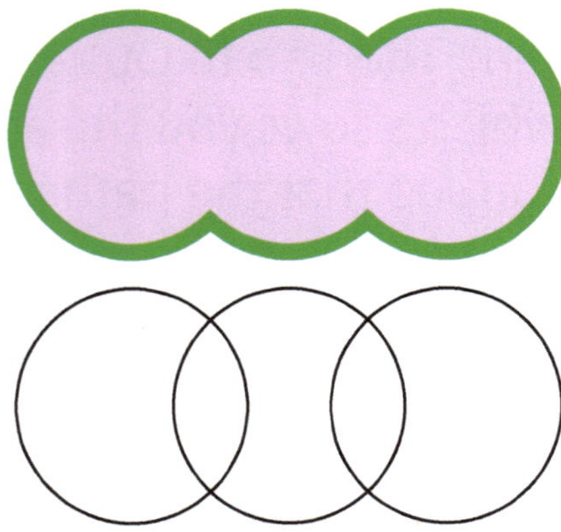

Unite **with** Option/Alt
in Outline View
(= shape = effect)

Now let's look at the Pathfinder Panel. The bottom row, which is labeled Pathfinders is straightforward: those items combine multiple paths in different ways to make a new path.

But the top row, labeled Shape Modes is tricky. First of all, what Illustrator is calling a shape here is simple an effect. Secondly, if you just click on one of these items you don't get a shape (effect) as you would expect. Instead you get a path. In order to get a shape you have to click with the Option/Alt modifier key, as the tool tip says. Confusing, huh? Anyway, as long as you know this, it becomes useful, and here's how:

In a complex design with many intersections, if you work around it using Unite without Option/Alt and you get to the end and then discover that you made a mistake near the start, which is probable, you have to start over. But if you made shapes rather than paths you can simply redo the problem area. You'll see how this works when we do this exercise.

1. Draw a round-cornered square like so with a stroke of 25 points at a size of about 2.25″.

2. Move a copy down so there is roughly the same space between the two as the width of the stroke.

3. Select them both and rotate a copy 90°. Group all four.

4. Draw a larger round-cornered square roughly from the center of the group approximately as shown. Give it roughly the same corner radius. Now center it exactly with the group of four using the Align Panel.

5. Outline strokes. Do Pathfinder > Divide as before. Put a 2 point white stroke on it to see where the divisions are. Remember, before Divide always see that the Pathfinder Option for *Divide and Outline Will Remove Unpainted Artwork* is checked.

6. Select all and Ungroup, since using Divide automatically groups. Now we will start to reunite the pieces. But this time we'll use the modifier key Option/Alt when clicking Pathfinder > Unite. Start working with the topmost object and go around it clockwise. As before, Unite the piece where the object goes **over** with the two adjacent pieces, as shown here in pink. Alternate over-under-over-under, etc.

7. Now do the same with the second small square (working clockwise). Select all the pieces shown here in green and then hit Unite with Option/Alt. It helps to color the pieces before you Unite to make it easier to see what you have. These need not be the final colors.

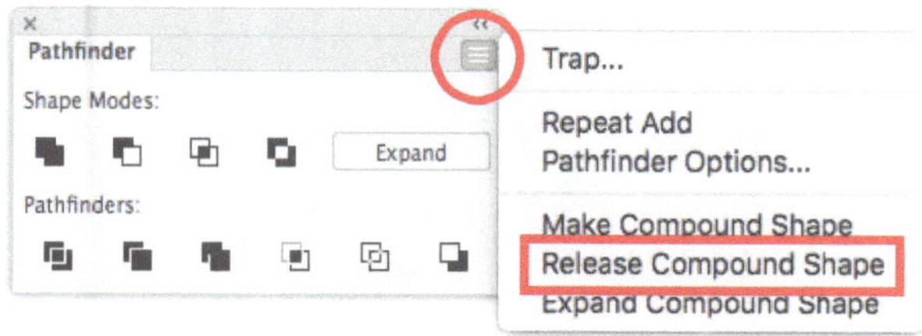

8. Now suppose you made a mistake on the green area and included a wrong piece or failed to include one. Here's how you can easily correct it: Select the green area with one click of the Selection Tool (because it is now grouped after Unite). Then, on the Pathfinder flyout menu do Release Compound Shape. It goes back to its Divided state and you can Unite again correctly.

9. Continue around with the other two small squares, and finally do the big square.

10. Add final color, as before: white stroke and colored fill, or colored stroke and fill, or fill with no stroke, or stroke with no fill. Rotate 45°. Done.

Another Complex Design using the Unite Shape Mode
Circles & Triangles

1. Draw a 3.5" diameter circle at 100% zoom. Gray fill and no stroke.

2. Draw a 21 point vertical black stroke and center it like so.

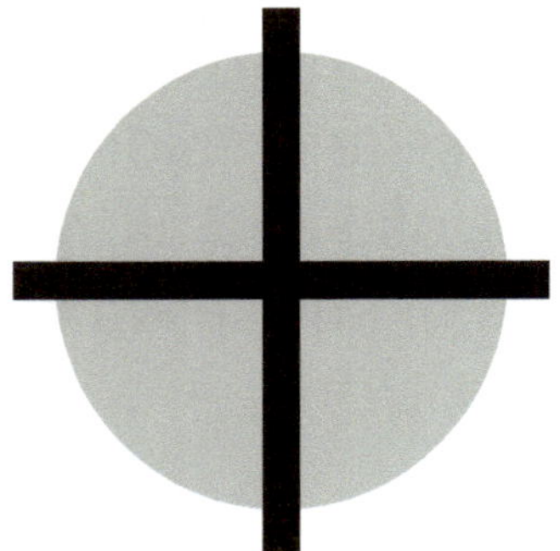

3. Rotate a copy of the stroke. Outline the two strokes.

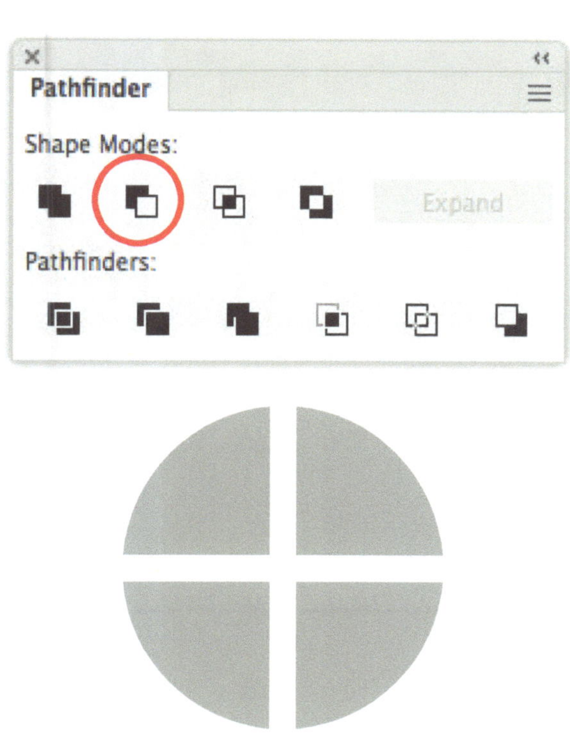

4. Select all and do Pathfinder > Minus Front (*without* the modifier key) to cut the outlined strokes out of the circle.

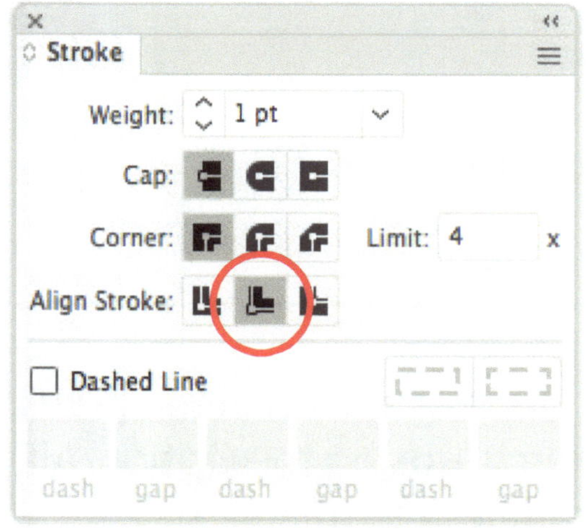

5. Change the fill to a 17 point stroke. Then Align Stroke to Inside.

6. Draw two circles with the same 21 point stroke, as shown. Center all.

7. Outline Strokes. Do Pathfinder > Divide. Then, as before, add a 2 point white stroke so you can see the divisions.

8. Unite as shown in the previous exercise, using the Option/Alt modifier key to make editable/reversible Compound Shapes (= effects). Rotate 45°. For logo *final files* it's a good idea to Expand the Shapes. You can do this either from the main menu (Object > Expand or Object > Expand Appearance), or from the Pathfinder flyout menu (Expand Compound Shape).

9. Add final color.

You can leave the white stroke.

Or use a different color stroke.

Or have no stroke.

Or have a stroke with no fill.

1. For the file, use Color Mode of CMYK. Draw a 1.5" circle with a 10 point stroke and no fill. Turn on Smart Guides. Precisely cut out a quarter of it on the anchor points. Add straight segments as shown.

2. Join the round and straight segments. Increase the stroke weight to 46 points.

3. With the Lasso Tool and the Direct Selection Tool adjust the design so it looks roughly like this. Then scale it to about 6" wide and change the stroke to 40 points.

4. Give the object a fill of CMYK 0-35-90-0 (yellow-orange). Zoom in. Turn on Smart Guides. Make a gray rectangle and precisely position it next to the intersection of two bands, as shown. The right side of the rectangle is at the start of the curve.

5. Put a gradient in the rectangle. Use a linear gradient. The right end is the same yellow-orange, to blend into the band. The left end of the gradient is the same color but with black added for the shadow effect. It makes it look like the upper band at the intersection is casting a shadow on the lower band that is going under. Do this in the Color Panel by moving the black (K) slider to about 20%.

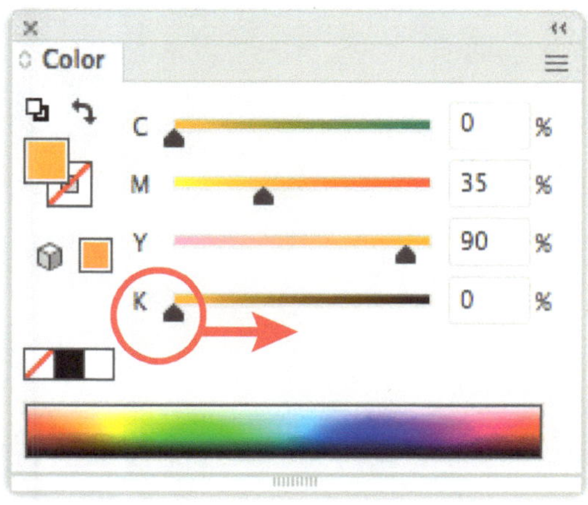

6. Using Smart Guides copy the gradient rectangle to the other intersections as shown. Keep the dark side of the gradient next to the intersection. Rotate the design as shown. Done. This could be a logo consisting of two script Ls.

On Logo Final Files

If you have white strokes in a design that is being used as a logo it's okay for a *draft* but no good for *a final file* because every time it's placed on a colored background the strokes will have to be changed to match the background. The way to get around this is to *delete* the strokes so that they are actually transparent and let the background color show through. Here's how to do it.

1. Check the stroke weight. It shouldn't be too small or it will plug up when printed at a small size. It should be at least 3 points when the logo is about 2" wide at 100% zoom. Make a note of the weight.

2. Give the stroke a color of None.

3. Move a copy off to the side. Then give it a fill of None and a stroke of the same weight as before in any contrasting color.

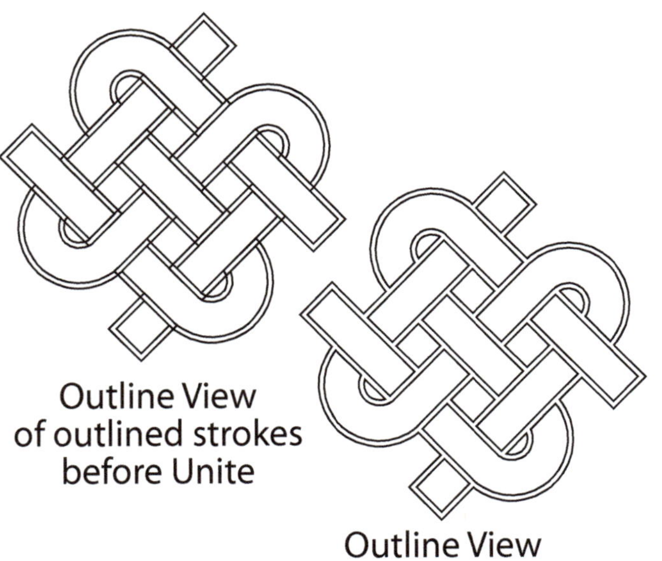

Outline View
of outlined strokes
before Unite

Outline View
of outlined strokes
after Unite

4. Outline Strokes. Then do Pathfinder > Unite (without the Option/Alt modifier key). Check in Outline View. You now have one unified object. The area that was strokes before is now a single filled object.

Outline View
after Unite

5. Copy the image from Step 2. Do Pathfinder > Unite (without the Option/Alt modifier key). Check in Outline View. It should look like this. If it didn't Unite perfectly you may have to move a few anchor points slightly to have all sections overlapping, then Unite again.

6. Here are the two images from Steps 4 and 5. Put the orange one on top in the stacking order, and center them.

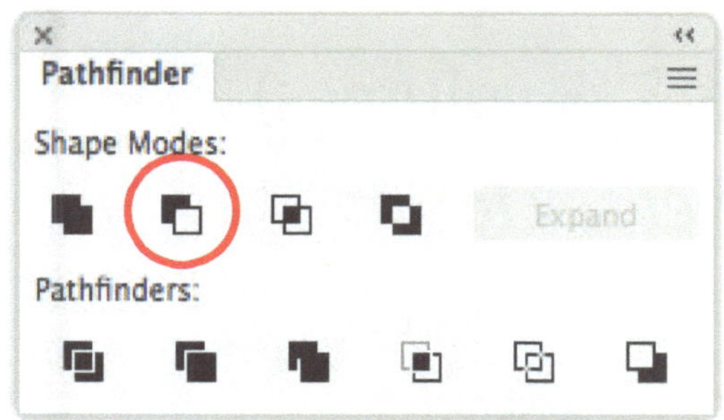

7. Select both, then do Pathfinder > Minus Front, without the modifier key. The orange object is now *subtracted* (cut away) from the blue, and what were white strokes before are now transparent. Check on a color background. Done.

Also by
Victor Langer

Logo Coloring Book

Crop Circle Coloring Book

Insect Coloring Book

Riddle-Poems for ages 3 to 7 (3 volumes)

1040 for Dogs, and other tax forms

Multiple-Universe Multiple-Choice

Geriacula, the Senile Vampire

www.ingramcontent.com/pod-product-compliance
Lightning Source LLC
Chambersburg PA
CBHW040205240726
48664CB00002B/843